MW01107666

GOD'S CHILDREN NEVER DIE

Richard E. Lauersdorf

Northwestern Publishing House
Milwaukee, Wisconsin

In loving memory
of my mother and father,
who brought me to Jesus
and who are now living with Jesus

Cover art by Gary Crabbe/Enlightened Images

Scripture is taken from the HOLY BIBLE, NEW INTERNATIONAL VERSION®. Copyright © 1973, 1978, 1984 by International Bible Society. Used by permission of Zondervan Publishing House. All rights reserved.

The "NIV" and "New International Version" trademarks are registered in the United States Patent and Trademark Office by International Bible Society. Use of either trademark requires the permission of International Bible Society.

All quoted hymns are taken from *Christian Worship: A Lutheran Hymnal.* © 1993 by Northwestern Publishing House.

Northwestern Publishing House
1250 N. 113th St., Milwaukee, WI 53226-3284
© 2003 by Northwestern Publishing House
www.nph.net
Published 2003
Printed in the United States of America
ISBN 0-8100-1555-2

Contents

1

GOD'S CHILDREN NEVER DIE

"I [Jesus] am the resurrection and the life. . . .
Whoever lives and believes in me will never die."

John 11:25,26 (NIV)

"Am I going to die?" the critically injured man gasped.
The pastor, hurriedly summoned to the hospital emergency
room, hesitated a moment before answering: "God's children never die." Then, with a gentle hold on the dying
man's hand and a strong hold on God's Word of Life, he led
that man to the Savior's atoning cross and emptied tomb.

Yes, God's children die. They are not exempt from the
Grim Reaper's scythe. For them too, life on this earth is
measured in days and months and years. For some the span
is long; for others, short. Age saps strength, disease does its
damage, and accidents take their toll for God's children also.
And in the end, their souls vacate the bodies that housed
them for their allotted time on earth.

God's children know they are going to die. Not too
many years into life, they bump up against death when pets
are lost or grandparents are taken from them. And once the
questions about death start, they never seem to stop.
Though believers know that eventually they will die, that
reality often only hovers on the horizon. However, when
death not only knocks at the door but barges right in to the

middle of life, reality hits hard. And the questions take on a more intense, searching tone.

In the face of death, God's children not only ask questions, they know where to find answers.

Thank God, they know the one who calls himself the Resurrection and the Life. Resurrection and life are so closely connected with Jesus that he calls them his own. Only he, who rose from the grave as proof that sin is canceled and death defeated, can offer resurrection to dying mortals. Only he, whose suffering, death, and resurrection paid for sin, can offer a life that never ends to those taking their last earthly breath.

So let the questions surface and the apprehensions bubble. By God's grace, believers look in faith to Jesus, the Resurrection and the Life. Because of him, they know God's children never die.

Prayer

Lord Jesus, you know my anguish and concern. Where can I turn? What can I do? Bring me close to you and to your promises. Help my heart hear and hold this blessed truth: in you I have a life that never ends but reaches its fullness with you in heaven. Amen.

2

LORD, IT'S NOT TRUE, IS IT?

The cords of death entangled me, the anguish of the grave came upon me; I was overcome by trouble and sorrow. Then I called on the name of the LORD: "O LORD, save me!"

Psalm 116:3,4 (NIV)

She just didn't want to talk about it. After her surgery the doctor had reported that death would be just a matter of time and that she had better get her house in order. But she didn't want to hear that. Nor should her family talk about it, not even her pastor.

Initially, denial can be a friend. Like sandbags used to line riverbanks, denial offers a buffer against the rising water. When the news is bad and the prognosis poor, we need time to catch our breath. Denial gives us time so that the numbness can wear off before we gear up for action.

Denial can also be a foe. When the river keeps rising, we invite disaster if we remain standing behind the sandbags instead of evacuating our houses. Then it's time to face reality and prepare for the inevitable. Continuing to deny the inescapable truth only deprives us of precious preparation time.

Facing death is an overwhelming burden. Numbness is natural—for God's children too. We shouldn't be surprised when they ask, "It's not true, Lord, is it?" The psalmist knew that feeling of shock. He first spoke of being entangled in death's cords and overcome with the grave's anguish. We can almost picture him throwing up his hands and saying, "Hold it, Lord. That can't be true, Lord." But then reality broke through the clouds of despair, and his prayer, "O LORD, save me!" went heavenward.

To deny the announcement of impending death is natural. To retreat into such denial from time to time is also natural. But to be stuck in such denial is like standing behind the sandbags and letting the rising river drown us. Far better to face the truth and evacuate to higher ground—to the Lord who alone saves. In his arms we find the power to walk onward, even into death's dark valley.

Prayer

Lord, you know how numb I am and how afraid I am of the truth. Help me look to you to find the strength I need. Help me find comfort in the words my loved ones and my pastor bring to me. Help me see my salvation in you. Amen.

3

LORD, HOW COULD YOU?

When Jesus saw her weeping, . . . he was deeply
moved in spirit and troubled.

John 11:33 (NIV)

He was angry—so angry that he didn't even want to talk.
He had been successful in his business, happy with his family, and active in his church. He had also been hit with a vir-
ulent and fatal form of cancer. The pastor, after unsuccessful
attempts at small talk, wisely urged, "Come on, John, spit it
out." And out it came. All of the man's frustration and
anger. Why had it happened to him? How could the Lord
do this when he still had so much to live for? How unfair
could it be?

Regardless of our age, dying incites anger within us.
Death robs us of family and friends, strips away our memories and dreams, and threatens us with the end of all we
hold precious. Who wouldn't be angry to be caught so
helplessly in death's trap? Perhaps even angry enough to
shake our fists at God and accuse him of making a mistake
or, at best, of not dealing fairly.

Death made Jesus angry too. As he stood before Lazarus'
grave, witnessing Martha's and Mary's grief, Jesus was visi-
bly distressed. Using a word that indicates anger, the sacred
record states, "he was deeply moved in spirit." It also says

he was "troubled," indicating agitation. Seldom in Scripture's record does the Savior show such deep emotions. But here in the midst of death's sad scene, he shows his anger over what sin has done to mankind. Physical death is the tragic result of sin. It brings the worst kind of sorrow and suffering with it.

So spit it out! Lash out at the suffering and separation that death brings. Such venting is normal for God's children. It isn't sinful. Don't be surprised, however, if you also find yourself lashing out with accusations against God. If we were super Christians, those accusing words, "How could you, Lord?" wouldn't rise from our lips. But since we are weak, they come. And when they do, we need to look again at our Savior Jesus.

Not only was he angry with sin's wages—namely, death—in divine love he did something about it. He raised his friend Lazarus to show that death was not the victor. If death is sin's wage, then life is sin's defeat. The Savior died our death and filled our grave to pay the penalty for all our sins, including our angry outbursts and anxious doubts. On Easter Sunday he rose again to show that death for us is not a tragic end but the glorious entrance into an eternal existence at his side. May that certain hope answer our questions and ease our anxieties.

Prayer

Lord, assure me through your Word that you hear and understand. Forgive me when I sin in anger, and comfort me with the sure hope of life in heaven with you. Grant this for your love's sake. Amen.

4

LORD, CAN WE MAKE A DEAL?

Teach us to number our days aright, that we may gain a heart of wisdom.

Psalm 90:12 (NIV)

What a pillar of faith and strength she was. Whenever her pastor visited, he was comforted by her trust in God's promises. In the face of impending death, she looked with confidence to the one who is the Resurrection and the Life. Then one day as their visit ended, she finally opened up. "If only the Lord would let me live long enough to see my last child married," she said wistfully. "Then I could die in peace."

In the face of death, it isn't unusual for believers to try to bargain with God. "If only God lets me live, I will do such and such with my life." "If only I could have a few more years, Lord, I would use them for you." "If only you delay my death, I will change this and that." Often the bargaining is sincere. Sometimes God even seems to accept the deal, and believers carry through on their promises. But often such bargaining is simply an attempt to delay the inevitable and to deny the unstoppable.

The psalmist didn't pray for an extension of life but for the right understanding of life. He wanted the Lord to teach him to number his days correctly and to view life as the time of preparation for heaven through Jesus. How long our time of grace extends is in the Lord's wise hands. What is done with that time of grace is in our hands.

When death draws near, God's children can pray about tomorrow. But we always leave the decision about the length of our lives in the Lord's hands. We are better off applying our hearts to wisdom today. We are better off using our remaining hours to grasp the best bargain the world has ever seen, the gift of eternal life a gracious God has freely prepared for us in the Savior Jesus Christ. Clutching that bargain, we're ready for death whenever it comes.

Prayer

Lord, you know the desires of my heart. You also know what is best for me and what is the best time for my departure. Teach me to trust you and to be satisfied with the number of days you grant me. In the days I have left, draw me closer to my Savior, the source of eternal life. Amen.

5

LORD, WHY HAVE YOU FORGOTTEN ME?

I say to God my Rock, "Why have you forgotten me?"

Psalm 42:9 (NIV)

I can still see the expression on our little son's face. While attending the state fair, we had stopped beside the long slide that people speed down on gunny sacks. It was a new attraction in those days. When we turned to go on, our son headed into the dense crowd in the opposite direction. All at once we realized that he wasn't with us, and we went scrambling for him. "Lost," that look on his little face said. "Forgotten."

People who are facing death know that feeling. Sometimes as they confront life's severest problem, even believers can't help thinking, "What's the use? Nothing seems to make any difference. Who cares?" They may not always say it, but sooner or later they think it. Even the strongest believers have days when they see only darkness and no stars—days when death seems to be only a dead end on life's road instead of the on-ramp to heaven's highway. So they clam up, silently turning their backs on loved ones and even on their God. Like the psalmist, they cry out in despair to their God, "Why have you forgotten me?"

"Forgotten me?" How could God ever do that? There he hangs on Calvary's cross, because he remembers me and dearly cares for me. There he sheds his precious blood for me that my sins might be forgiven. There he gives his life for me that I might share his life in heaven. He will not leave me helpless or hopeless, not even in the face of life's greatest problem. Underneath me at the moment of death will be his everlasting arms, to cradle me and carry me safely home.

When impending death pulls us into the pit of depression, doctors may help by prescribing medicine. But only Jesus, the rock of our salvation, can revive the flagging spirits of our souls and raise our eyes of faith to heaven's shores.

Prayer

Lord, I know you understand when I feel down and depressed. Don't leave me alone in this wilderness, but rescue me by assuring me of your saving love. Let your Holy Word and Holy Supper revive my sinking spirits and ready me for my departure. This I ask for your love's sake. Amen.

6

LORD, AREN'T YOU LISTENING?

O LORD, hear my prayer, listen to my cry for mercy;
in your faithfulness and righteousness come to
my relief.

Psalm 143:1 (NIV)

Her hospital stay had been long and painful. As her
strength waned, it was obvious to all, including her, that
death was near. After I finished the bedside devotion with
prayer, she was strangely silent. Finally she looked up at me
and said what was on her mind. "Pastor," she asked, "is he
really listening?"

The psalmist asked the same question. Behind his plea
for the Lord to hear his prayer was the feeling that the Lord
wasn't listening. Those who face life's greatest battle know
the feeling. Again and again they've sent their prayers to the
Lord of mercy. Again and again they've pleaded for his help.
Again and again they've waited for his answer. But the pain
continues. The disease keeps ravaging their bodies. The
prognosis gets no better. The end approaches. And the question arises, also in believers' hearts and minds, "Lord, aren't
you listening?"

The psalmist answered his own question. "In your faithfulness and righteousness come to my relief," he prayed.
Though believers waver at times because of the pressures of

living and dying, they know what their God is like. The one to whom we pray is a faithful God who keeps his promises. He is a righteous God, who always deals fairly with us.

If we have any doubts, we need only raise our eyes to his Son's cross. The promise he made to our sin-ruined parents in the Garden of Eden, he kept in full as he hung his Son on the cross, in total payment for sin. He will also keep the promises he has made for our earthly journeys, even when those journeys take a painful route through the valley of the shadow of death. He will not let us walk into that unknown valley alone. He will send his Son, whom we know and trust, to walk with us—even to carry us safely through the valley to heaven's shore. The time when that walk should take place, we leave in his hands. We pray about it. In our humanity, we even tell him what we would like. But then we lean back into his all-knowing embrace and accept the answer his loving wisdom sends.

When believers talk to their Father in prayer, they not only tell him their anxieties, they also listen for his answers.

Prayer

Lord, I know you hear me when I pray. Please forgive me when, in my weakness, I doubt or wonder. Please hold me closer through your Word. Help me raise my fears and tears to you in prayer, telling you my needs and then hearing your answers. Amen.

7

LORD, WHY IS IT SO HARD TO TALK ABOUT IT?

Then Israel said to Joseph, "I am about to die, but God will be with you."

Genesis 48:21 (NIV)

"So what are you really thinking?" asked the pastor. He had just finished his devotion at the bedside of a believer who was terminally ill. Silence had hung in the air for a while. Then the pastor wisely asked his question. With a little prodding the dying Christian opened up, and her concerns came tumbling out.

How hard it is to talk about dying! Some doctors don't like to use the word. Instead, they find sugar-coated substitutes. As death draws near, their brief daily calls to the patient's room become even briefer. Relatives and friends don't like to talk about death either. When they run out of things to say about the weather or current events, they sit in silence or find a reason to leave. If a dying loved one should even bring up the subject, they try to shush him up. And the dying person? For him the subject can be difficult too. But so necessary!

What better remedy is there for our fears about death than to speak about them with believers who love us? The dying lady found that out as she poured out her heart to her pastor that day. In response he could validate her fears and then offer the antidote found in the living Savior. What better way to be assured that our loved ones will be all right when we are gone than to bring the subject up with them? That's what the pastor urged the lady to do the next time her family came. Not everyone will want to listen to such talk, but the discussion is necessary, both for those who talk and those who listen.

And what better preacher is there than a dying believer? Jacob, whose other name was Israel, knew this. He spoke plainly to his beloved son Joseph. "I am about to die," he said, stating a fact both of them already knew. "But God will be with you," he went on, stressing another fact that Joseph also needed to know. Father and son could talk about death—and both would benefit. The father could also talk to his son about the one who would remain with him, namely, the Lord, whose promises are new every morning. Eloquent are the words a dying believer speaks about his hope in the Lord.

Prayer

Lord, thank you for talking to me about death and life. Without your words, I would be lost and hopeless at a time like this. Help me now speak about death and life with my loved ones. I need their comfort and assurance, and they need my openness. Amen.

8

LORD, IS IT ALL RIGHT TO CRY?

Jesus wept.

John 11:35 (NIV)

"God will wipe away every tear from their eyes."

Revelation 7:17 (NIV)

"I just can't help it," the burly lawman apologized. When his pastor took his hand in that hospital room, the patient had burst into tears. Exploratory surgery had uncovered the worst kind of news. The malignancy had spread throughout his body. Surgery wouldn't help; the future was bleak. The believer who was so used to being in charge was now helpless.

Jesus wept too, for a different reason. At the grave of his dear friend Lazarus, the Savior burst into tears. Like a tornado, death had swept through Bethany, leaving in its aftermath a lifeless body and survivors filled with overwhelming sorrow and helplessness. When the God-man Jesus saw the ravages of death that day, his eyes flooded over. But his tears were not tears of helplessness. The lawman's tears didn't need to be either.

"Go ahead and cry," the pastor told that lawman. "You're in good company. Jesus cried too. He knows what you're feeling." Then the pastor told him about Jesus' other tears, the ones only the Savior could shed. In the shadows of Gethsemane, Jesus wept heavy tears because of the load his Father had asked him to carry. The sins of the world were on his shoulders. Their payment would pin him to that cruel cross and plunge him into the pains of hell. But when it was all done, he could declare, "It is finished." Sin was paid for. Death had been defeated. Because of Jesus, our tears in the face of death are no longer a sign of helplessness. Rather, they show how human we are and how real death is.

So go ahead and cry. Death, the horrible wages of sin, brings tears to our eyes. But don't let the tears blur your view of the blessed scene awaiting you in heaven. There his hands, once pierced with nails, will be the soft tissue to wipe away the last trace of your tears.

Prayer

Lord, thank you for showing me that it's all right to cry. Give me strength so that my tears are never bitter or hopeless tears but, rather, tears that express my pain and anguish. Help me see through these tears so that I can recognize your salvation and the beautiful scene that awaits me in heaven. There I shall weep no more. Amen.

9

Lord, Remind Me I'm Never Alone

"Never will I leave you; never will I forsake you."

Hebrews 13:5 (NIV)

Dying is a lonely business. It's one of the two times in life when you are really alone. Though your parents and the hospital staff were around you when you were born, you entered this world alone. When death approaches, people may be all around again. Yet you will exit this world alone. No one can walk with you at that final moment.

So you feel lonely. Almost enough at times to roll yourself up into the fetal position and turn your face toward the wall. "Leave me alone," you feel like telling well-meaning loved ones and visitors. "Don't bother me by talking about things that no longer are of interest to me," you shout inside yourself. "They just don't know how lonely I am," you groan.

Sometimes it's worse than at other times. In the middle of the night when it seems that you're the only one awake, death's reality looms even darker. The constant sounds of the machines you're hooked up to offer little comfort. They just emphasize that death is near. How alone you are!

Not really. Little third-grade Angie had it right. Hospitalized at Children's Hospital, Angie faced her fifth (and fatal) surgery for a recurring brain tumor. After fastening a glow-in-the-dark scene of Jesus' blessing the little children to her bed, I asked her, "Angie, do you know who that little one in Jesus' arm is? That's you." As I got ready to leave her room, she reached up to kiss my cheek and then pointed, "I'm not alone. He's holding me."

God helps us remember that we are never alone. How can he who has bought us with his life's blood, drop us when the going gets tough? How can he who has guaranteed to be with us always, tell us in our last minutes that his warranty doesn't cover death? When he says "Never will I leave you; never will I forsake you," we can count on it, even in the moment of death.

Prayer

Lord, how alone I feel! No one knows what it's like, not even my closest loved ones. Hold me close. Let me feel your everlasting love. Let me see the proof of your love in the form of your suffering and death for my sins. Let me then see that you are always present at my side. Amen.

10

LORD, REMIND ME OF WHO I AM

"Fear not, for I have redeemed you; I have summoned you by name; you are mine."

Isaiah 43:1 (NIV)

When the world tumbles in around us, it's easy to forget who we are. "Pastor, sometimes I feel like I'm just another blob, just some nameless, faceless entity in this huge world," said a shut-in who was not long for this world. It's true that the Lord has more than six billion others to take care of. Humanly speaking, he must be more than busy, mopping up the spills sinners cause and keeping the complex universe spinning smoothly. Could it be that he forgets or doesn't have time for us, especially in the hour of need?

Let's ask him. After all, we need to hear it from his own lips. "Don't worry," he says. "I have redeemed you. I've bought and paid for you with the most precious thing I have, the blood of my own Son. I put the sign of his redeeming cross on you at your baptism, telling the devil that now you belong to me. I'm not about to toss you aside now as though you were no longer of any value to me."

"Don't worry," he says further. "I have summoned you by name." In this world we may be no more than a number. Social security numbers, zip code numbers, hospital identification numbers—that's how people refer to us. But our God calls us by name. Think about what that means. We are not just nameless, faceless children to him. We are children he knows by name—each one of us. He knows our heartaches and heartbreaks, our tears and trials, our conditions and needs. He knows how much our shoulders can carry. He knows when and how to strengthen our shoulders under a cross—and when and how to remove that cross, lest we stumble under its weight. He also knows the manner and time of death that is good for each one of us, and he carries out his plan accordingly.

"You are mine," he concludes. When a lover says to his beloved, "You are mine," everyone knows what he means. Nothing is more precious, nothing gets more of his love, nothing can separate the two of them. Yet because people are mortal, the time of separation comes. When the almighty God says, "You are mine," that lasts forever. Each of his children is covered with his Son's blood. Each is a precious jewel that will shine in his heavenly crown. Each is guaranteed safe handling until it is time to stand with his heavenly family.

Let's not forget, though, God doesn't make such promises because of who and what we are. Sinners deserve nothing from him except punishment. Such precious promises come only because of who and what God is. He is a God whose love is undeserved and unending, a God who not only made us precious through the Savior but deals with us accordingly—even in the time of dying and at the hour of death.

Prayer

Lord, do you still remember me? Do you still care for me? Please forgive me when I wonder in my weakness. Draw me back to your Son's cross to see how much you love me. Assure me that your love never changes but always covers me, even in the hour of death. Amen.

11

LORD, I CAN'T, BUT YOU CAN

Out of the depths I cry to you, O LORD; O Lord, hear my voice. Let your ears be attentive to my cry for mercy.

Psalm 130:1,2 (NIV)

Only a few wheezing words, that's all he could muster. Lying in the veteran's hospital—this would be the last time—he was hooked up to several machines. Lungs, ruined during World War II, wouldn't make it much longer. "Pastor, I can't pray," his lips formed the words. He was not only incapable of getting the words out, but his mind and body were too exhausted to concentrate on prayer. "You don't need words," the pastor replied. "Just whisper in your heart. All you need to say is 'Lord, I can't, but you can.'"

In our verse the unnamed psalmist said the same thing, though with different words. Could it be that the Lord didn't record the name of the psalmist because he wants us to make these words our own? Each of us has been plunged into his or her own depths. What problem can be deeper than a sickbed and impending death? Only those who are hooked up to machines and are nearing the end know how deep that hole can be. Only those whose strength fails and whose lips can no longer form the words know how helpless they feel and how powerless they are even to pray.

For those in the depths of suffering, there is no better prayer than "Lord, I can't, but you can." Lord, I can't do anything to relieve my heavy pain, restore my failing strength, or ready myself for the dark road ahead. Lord, I can't do anything to make life last another second, even if I wanted to. Lord, I can't do anything to erase my worries about what will happen to the loved ones I leave behind. And Lord, I can't do anything to ease my fears as death's fist knocks insistently on life's door.

"But you can, Lord." That's the answer I need. You have already pulled me up from the pit of my sins by plunging your own Son into hell's pains for me. You have already cleansed me with his precious blood and clothed me with his robe of righteousness. Your love has done what I can't do—it has written my name in your book of life in heaven. And it has promised to let nothing, not even my death, erase that entry.

Now, Lord, please hear my voice, even when I can't form the words. Please assure me that your mercy covers me, both soul and body, and that it always will.

Prayer

Lord, I'm so tired, so weary, so helpless. You know how I feel and what I need. Through your Word show me again what you have done for me in Jesus. Let my salvation, worked by your love, assure me that you can handle everything else in my life, even the journey at the end of my life. In Jesus' name I ask this. Amen.

12

LORD, CHANGE ME FROM AFRAID TO APPREHENSIVE

Jesus answered, "I am the way. . . . No one comes to
the Father except through me."

John 14:6 (NIV)

"I'm afraid. There, I finally said it. I'm afraid." It took
some courage for the patient to admit this to her pastor. It
also took confidence that he wouldn't scold her but would
understand. Usually we cry into our pillows in the dark
when no one can hear us. We keep that stiff upper lip so
others won't think ill of us. But in trying to hide our fear,
we only encourage it to deepen its shadows.

Taking her hand, the pastor asked, "Are you afraid of
death or are you apprehensive?" Then he went on to
explain. As children, when we first attempted to ride a bicy-
cle, it wasn't with fear but with apprehension. We wanted
to ride but didn't know how. When we were teenagers, we
went on our first dates. We were jittery, not because we
were afraid, but because we hadn't done that before. On
our wedding days, it wasn't fear but apprehension that
made us nervous. Would our love be lifelong? How could
we know without trying? When the first baby was on the
way, it was the same thing—not fear but apprehension
because of the unknown.

The patient was nodding in agreement. "So it is with death," the pastor continued. "It's a brand-new experience for us. We have never walked that way before. No one has ever returned to tell us how it goes. Of course we're apprehensive. Of course we have all sorts of questions, all sorts of thoughts. And there's nothing wrong with them."

Then the pastor pointed her to the answers for her questions. Though God's children don't know what death will be like or how they will face it, they do know two important truths. They know that death leads to heaven. And they know that Jesus is the only way there. The Savior himself has told us, so we know it is true. "I am the way," he said. He not only shows or leads us on the way. He is the way. He is the road our feet of faith must travel if we want to reach heaven. He also has told us where he leads—to the Father. That's what heaven really is—being forever with the Father, who made us and redeemed us. To be eternally safe in his house, secure in his family, serving him without sin, that's what heaven is. Though we don't know what death will be like, by God's grace we do know where it will take us and how to get there.

Please, Lord, let my thoughts be, "Afraid? No! Apprehensive? Yes!" By showing me Christ's promises again, may the Spirit change my anxiety into anticipation.

Prayer

Lord, I've talked to you about my concerns. I've carried my anxious questions to you. Show me the answers I need so that I won't be overcome with fear. Show me my Savior's loving face and his promise of your eternal home. Help me be brave enough to talk about my concerns also with those near and dear to me. I need their encouragement, and they need your answers too. In the name of Jesus, who is the way to heaven, I ask this. Amen.

13

LORD, REMIND ME THAT IT'S NOT HOW LONG, BUT HOW

I tell you, now is the time of God's favor, now is the day of salvation.

2 Corinthians 6:2 (NIV)

"My suitcase is packed," Brian said. Bone cancer had hit this young college student for the second time. No longer was there any hope of returning to school, reclaiming his place on the baseball team, or resuming even a semblance of normal life. In fact, there in his bedroom in his parent's house, I had just communed him for what was to be the last time. Gripping my hand my former student said, "Don't worry about me. My suitcase is packed, just as you told us in confirmation class."

Life is the time God grants us to pack our suitcase for heaven. It's the span of time God measures as the opportunity for each person to learn of the Savior. How long or short that time span extends is in the Lord's hands. For some it's much longer than the proverbial threescore years and ten. For others, as for Brian, it is as short as 22 years. The question isn't how long life will last. It's whether life will have served its purpose. Did the individual use life to pack the suitcase for heaven? When the giver of life knocks on the door, the user of that life can't shout, "Just a minute. I'm not finished packing." Then either the suitcase contains Jesus or it doesn't. A person's eternal future depends on the answer.

It hurts to have life snuffed out before it has a chance to really shine. It hurts to have dreams left unfulfilled, futures left unrealized, potential left untapped. It hurts parents to lose the children they showered with their love, the precious children they viewed as their replacements. But it would hurt so much more if God's purpose for that life was unfulfilled, if that short life was not used to pack the suitcase for heaven.

"Now is the time of God's favor." Now, while we're still breathing and our hearts are still beating—labored though both may be—now is our time to be prepared for heaven through faith in Jesus the Savior. Then, when our last moments come, by his grace and favor, it'll be the best day of our lives, the day of our salvation.

Prayer

Lord, I had so much living left to do. You know my dreams and hopes, my desires for the future. And now, Lord, I see them all going up in smoke. Please take my hand and lead me to Jesus. Show me that in him I have all I need, even a future filled with hopes beyond imagination. Let his saving arms hold me close as my last hour approaches, that I may be ready to stand in glory before your throne. Amen.

14

LORD, HELP ME MEND THE FENCES

Bear with each other and forgive whatever grievances you may have against one another. Forgive as the Lord forgave you.

Colossians 3:13 (NIV)

Ramón was so glad his son had arrived in time. Years before, he and his son had had a falling out as they tried to run a business together. Money can do that to people. So can a sharp tongue that so quickly wounds and a thin skin that is so easily scratched. For years they had barely spoken to each other. Then Ramón had learned he was dying. He knew he needed to see his son. "Call him," he had begged his wife. "I just have to mend fences with him before I die."

Any time in life is a good time to forgive whatever grievances we may have against one another. Our Savior commanded his loving followers to do that. And our loving Savior did that and still does that for us each day. What if we had to die with all our sins still piled up before us? What if our closing eyes saw only righteous anger on the face of God? Thank God for his full and free forgiveness on which to pillow our hearts when death's day comes.

But the business of forgiving can be so difficult at times. How deeply we may have been hurt or may have hurt someone else! How fresh the wounds we may have inflicted on others or others may have inflicted on us. How hard it is to speak the words "I'm sorry" or "I forgive you"! So we journey on, trying to forget the gaps in the fences of life, leaving them unmended. Even when death approaches, we have a hard time backing up to those broken fences and doing something about them. But we miss something extremely important if we don't.

Ramón and his son had time together. With some difficulty they began to talk about what each had done. They ended up in tears, arms wrapped around each other, expressing love and forgiveness. Later that day they received the Lord's body and blood in his Holy Supper for the assurance of their forgiveness. The pastor saw the joy they shared.

Do you have any fences to mend? Now's the time—while there still is time. Reach up to the Savior for his rich forgiveness. Then reach out with forgiveness to one another.

Prayer

Lord, I don't know how you do it, how you can forgive me sin after sin, day after day. But I'm so glad you do. Without your forgiveness, I cannot die in peace. But, Lord, I don't know how I can forgive those with whom I've had problems. Help me, Lord, to feel your forgiveness more richly so that I can forgive others more readily. Amen.

15

LORD, THANK YOU FOR SUPPER

"Take and eat; this is my body. . . . Drink from it, all of you. This is my blood of the covenant, which is poured out for many for the forgiveness of sins."

Matthew 26:26-28 (NIV)

"Pastor, may I have the Lord's Supper?" the elderly lady asked. The next morning she faced the surgeon's knife, and she had a pretty good idea what the outcome would be. When we had finished, she said, "Thank you, Pastor. And thank you, Lord. I needed him to tell me that all is well regardless of what tomorrow brings." Less than a week later, I was able to be the Lord's instrument again, offering his aged child the very body and blood used in payment for her sin. Though she couldn't speak as she lay in the intensive care unit, her eyes nodded their appreciation for her Lord's rich gift.

We can die without receiving Holy Communion. The Lord's Supper is not a magical send-off to heaven. Many believers die without having the time or the opportunity to receive his Supper. Nor does Holy Communion offer a different kind of forgiveness. There is only one kind of forgiveness, the same one found in the written and spoken gospel message. The difference lies in the way the Savior presents his forgiveness in his Supper.

In his Supper, the Savior comes to each believer in a uniquely personal way, as he did to that elderly lady. He put his arm on her shoulder, looked her lovingly in the eye, and assured her, "Here is my body. I gave it for you. Here is my blood. I shed it for you. Your sins are forgiven. You can go home, even to your eternal home, in peace."

Who can be more hungry for the Lord's forgiveness than dying sinners? Who can appreciate more deeply this wondrous meal than those about to meet their Lord? Dying is an individual matter; so is the need for forgiveness. Thank God he offers just that in his blessed sacrament.

Prayer

This feast is manna, wealth abounding
Unto the poor, to weak ones pow'r,
To angels joy, to hell confounding,
And life for me in death's dark hour.
Lord, may your body and your blood
Be for my soul the highest good! Amen.

16

LORD, TELL ME AGAIN AND AGAIN THAT YOU LOVE ME

For I am convinced that neither death nor life, . . . nor anything else in all creation, will be able to separate us from the love of God that is in Christ Jesus our Lord.

Romans 8:38,39 (NIV)

Can you even imagine a hospital room without love? Dying with no loved ones at your side? No loved ones with whom you can reminisce and to whom you can give last reminders? No loved ones from whom you can draw comfort—from their words and from their presence at your side? No loved ones to buoy you up when the waves grow steeper?

Then imagine dying without the one who loves us the most. About his love there can be no doubt. He's already proved it by placing his own Son into our skin, under our sins, and through hell's suffering. With a love we'll never fully understand, even if we live to be two hundred, our God has prepared salvation for us and provided a life that never ends. No wonder the Bible uses a special word for his love. In the original language spoken by Jesus and the apostles, the word refers to a love that is completely undeserved. It's a love that loves the unlovable, a love that doesn't depend on us but depends totally on him.

As Paul describes God's wondrous love in Christ, he assures us that nothing can separate us from that love. The devil would like to use death like a crowbar to pry us loose from God. He whispers in our ears that God is too far away and that his love is too feeble to hold us during that last dark hour. And sometimes we nod our heads in agreement. Or we are tempted to forget that the glue which holds us tightly to God comes from him, not from us.

So, please, Lord, tell me again and again of your great love for me in Christ. I can't die in peace without your love. Point me to those "love" passages in your Holy Word that assure me that you forgive me when I sin, seek me when I stray, hold me when I'm weak, and that you will receive me into glory when I die. Let these words I learned in childhood be my prayer and my confidence: "Jesus loves me, this I know, for the Bible tells me so."

Prayer

Lord, thank you for the loved ones you have placed at my side. Their presence and comforting words mean so much to me. Even more, Lord, thank you for the love that causes you to hold me. Don't let the pains of my last hours rip me loose from Jesus. Keep me ever close to him, and assure me that you love me and that you will bring me safely home to heaven. Amen.

17

LORD, TEACH ME HOW TO FIGURE

I consider that our present sufferings are not worth
comparing with the glory that will be revealed in us.

Romans 8:18 (NIV)

"Tell me again about that 8:18," the burn victim
pleaded. When his house went up in flames, he had been
burned to within an inch of his life. Soon even that inch
would be taken away, and his pain would be over. In the
meantime, the pain was severe. Never completely dulled by
the medications, it always came roaring back to toss his
body and test his soul.

What could his pastor tell him? On his first visit, he had
read Paul's words from Romans 8:18. Guided by the Spirit,
his pastor had explained that believers need to learn a new
way of figuring. Believers need to place the pains of this life
on one end of God's scale and the glory waiting in heaven
on the other—then see which way the scale tips. Life's
pains, as severe and unbearable as they might seem, are
only for a while. The eternal glory awaiting us in our heavenly home far outweighs them all. The believer in that burn
center needed to hear that. The words of Romans 8:18
didn't take away his horrible pain, but they did point his
eyes where they needed to be.

What a burden pain can be. Only those enduring its never-ending waves know how pain can dissolve their strength, etch deep wounds on their spirits, and eat away at their souls. Whether they are unbelievers or believers, those who suffer pain know how great the burden can be. But only believers know 8:18. God has raised our eyes to the ultimate end, that home he has prepared for us, where we will live with the one who loves us and has saved us. Though in our pain we can't see the glory he has waiting for us, in faith we trust it is there. Because we see the glorious end of the journey, we keep walking onward, even though the hills are steep and the valleys deep.

And we have one more comfort. We can look at our Savior in the garden, wrestling with pain so severe it caused him to sweat drops of blood. We can see his anguish on the cross, as his blood stained Calvary's sand. We can hear his exhausted cry from that cross, "I thirst." And we know that Jesus knows. He knows what pain is like. Jesus knows what our pain is like. Jesus not only knows our pain, but he will strengthen us for our walk through pain to the promised place of glory at his side.

Prayer

Lord, I don't know if I can stand this pain. It just keeps washing over me, one wave after another. What am I going to do, Lord? Oh, please teach me how to figure correctly. Teach me how to weigh heaven's glory, prepared for me by Jesus, over against the troubles I now face. Show me his suffering in Gethsemane and on Calvary. Help me to remember that he feels my pain and that he knows how to help me endure. In his name I come to you. Amen.

18

LORD, KEEP ME HOPING

Praise be to the God and Father of our Lord Jesus Christ! In his great mercy he has given us new birth into a living hope through the resurrection of Jesus Christ from the dead, and into an inheritance that can never perish, spoil or fade—kept in heaven for you.

1 Peter 1:3,4 (NIV)

Hope is essential in life—especially in times of sickness. No matter how uncertain the future or how disappointing the predicted outcome may be, doctors still try to hold out hope. Without hope there is little spirit for the fight, little energy to endure. Doctors also remember that they have miscalculated in the past and that hope can prove their predictions wrong.

But what happens when there is no more hope? When all the medications have been tried without success? When surgery cannot stop cancer's insidious growth? When the damage caused by an accident cannot be repaired? When the heart muscles cannot be rejuvenated? What then?

The pastor followed the doctor into Tonya's room. Just an hour earlier, her physician had told her the "bad" news. Nothing more could be done. It was just a matter of time. Her family had gathered around her, but everyone had trouble finding words to speak. There didn't seem to be any hope in that hospital room.

Or was there? The pastor read Peter's inspired words about the "living hope" our God has prepared for us through his Son's death and resurrection. As he read, hope's light shone again in that room. He read about the heavenly inheritance that can never perish, spoil, or fade, and hope's light shone even brighter. Earthly hopes pop up for a while, then just as quickly fade away. Our lives endure for a bit, but they eventually expire. One by one our earthly hopes disappear or are taken from us. But the hope a loving God has given us in Christ lasts forever. Not even death can rob the believer of the hope kept in heaven for us.

Of this living hope we can never hear too much. Its sure message gives us guidance in life and a guarantee in death.

Prayer

Lord, helper of the helpless and hope of the hopeless, shine in my heart with the promises of my inheritance in heaven. I cannot go on without the hope those promises give. Please forgive me when that hope fades and I begin to give up. Please let your Word light the way, so that I can walk forward with eternal hope. Strengthen me with the conviction that whether I live or die, I belong to you. Amen.

19

LORD, WHO WILL TAKE CARE OF THEM?

He tends his flock like a shepherd: He gathers the
lambs in his arms and carries them close to his heart;
he gently leads those that have young.

Isaiah 40:11 (NIV)

Sam was worried. Looking at his wife and young family,
he couldn't help worrying. Yes, he had some insurance.
Social security would fill some of the gaps until the children were older. But what about the mortgage payments?
What about protecting his wife or guiding his boys until
they could be on their own? Sam wouldn't be around much
longer to take care of them. And his question, "Who will
take care of them?" bothered him deeply.

The Lord does not show believers where the path
ahead leads nor how steep it will be. He does, however,
remind his flock who it is that takes care of them. Though
Isaiah's picture of shepherds, sheep, and lambs is not
as familiar for us today, we can still catch its comfort.
Gullible adult sheep will find guidance under the shepherd's care. The weakest newborn lambs will find safety in
the shepherd's arms and comfort near his heart. He will
tenderly lead the parents, who, like ewes, are nursing the
young. He will gently care for the little ones, who, like
lambs, are being nourished.

In the arms of such a gentle Shepherd, all members of the flock are safe. Those who are about to depart this life find their confidence in the bleeding Shepherd. They fall asleep in Jesus' wounds, where pardon for their sins abounds. Those who survive find their confidence in the Shepherd, who will lead and feed them. He who laid down his life for them will also lead them where they need to go, providing the green pastures and still waters along the way.

This loving Shepherd understands those times when, in the difficult moments of life, we wonder about the way he leads us. He not only understands, but with his promises, he wraps his caring arms even more tightly around us. In this Shepherd we find the answers to our concerns for loved ones who will remain after we are gone. Into his gentle yet powerful arms, we entrust our family for safekeeping.

Prayer

Lord, you know how concerned I am about my family. I won't be here to love them, to take care of them, or to guide them. What am I going to do? Who will take care of them? O Lord, show me again your Shepherd's heart. Show me again your Shepherd's strong arm. Show me again the love that moves both your heart and arm to care for the young and old in your flock. Let the care that surrounds me in my last hour surround them also in the days and years ahead. Amen.

20

LORD, CAN I HEAR YOUR ASSURANCE AGAIN?

You will again have compassion on us; you will tread our sins underfoot and hurl all our iniquities into the depths of the sea.

Micah 7:19 (NIV)

"Will you please close the door?" Adeline asked her pastor. Both knew death was near. She had obviously been listening as he brought the sweet news of forgiveness and certain victory over death through the Savior. But there was something more. And in that private room, she opened her heart, confessing the youthful sin by which she had shattered her marriage. For years guilt had kept her away from church. Even after she came back, that sin rubbed her conscience sore and rattled like some scary skeleton in her heart. Now she needed to know. Had God forgiven her? Could she die in peace? Or would she have to carry that sin before his judgment throne?

How accurate are the devil's files in which he records our sins! How adept he is at dipping into those files at just the right time and drawing out just the right one in order to accuse us! As death draws closer, so does the old evil foe. "You think God wants you," he whispers. "You and I both remember what you have done. Don't you think he remembers too?" Each sin is serious in the eyes of our holy God.

Each sin earns the fires of hell as its wage. But some sins etch our memories more deeply and emerge to trouble our hearts more energetically. Adeline had her own. So does each of us.

How we need the assurance God gave Israel through his prophet Micah—even more so on our deathbeds! Forgiveness is real, as if God has stomped those sins into dust so that they can no longer rise to haunt us. Forgiveness is real, as if God has submerged our sins in the deepest part of the sea so they can never be found or remembered again. His forgiveness is real because the payment was real. Through his Son's death on the cross, he paid for all of our sins, including those that especially trouble us. Will he now raise these sins up from the dust or reach down for them in the depths of the sea? Jesus' payment for our sins makes that not only unnecessary but impossible.

"Adeline," the pastor said, "remember, when Jesus said 'It is finished,' he meant also the payment for the sin that is troubling you. And, Adeline," he continued, "remember that when God plunges our sins into the depths of the sea, he also puts up a sign telling us, 'No fishing allowed.'"

Prayer

Lord, you've told me again and again through my baptism, through your Word, and through the Holy Supper that you have forgiven me. But, Lord, I need to hear again that your forgiveness covers that "special" sin that troubles me. I need to be assured, in this last hour, that your Son's blood has washed my iniquity from me. Hold his atoning cross even more closely before my closing eyes. Shout his victorious claim, "It is finished," even more loudly into my fading ears. Help me die at peace with you and with myself. For his love's sake, I ask this. Amen.

21

LORD, WHAT'S IT LIKE ON THE OTHER SIDE?

"They will be his people, and God himself will be with them and be their God. He will wipe every tear from their eyes. There will be no more death or mourning or crying or pain, for the old order of things has passed away."

Revelation 21:3,4 (NIV)

"Tell me about heaven," the dying Christian asked. Ready to leave this world, robed in her Savior's blood and righteousness, she wanted a preview of the place where she was going. In response, her pastor read the words of our verse. Like a travel brochure, those words depict an inviting picture of a beautiful place. Unlike some travel brochures, the words are not a flowery exaggeration or misleading traveler's tale.

What's it like on the other side, that better side of life we call heaven? "No more pain," John answers. On this earth we so often wrestle with and grow weary under a burden of pain. So often, particularly near the end, life seems to be one painful step after the other. "No more death," he also says. We've been waiting for the day when "heav'n's morning breaks, and earth's vain shadows flee."

"No more crying," he adds. No more tears inside our torn hearts or outside on our pillows because of the bumps and bruises of life.

"For the old order of things has passed away," John explains. "No more sin," he is really saying. When sin entered the world, it carried a suitcase filled with pain, death, and sorrow. When the saints stand before God, washed in the blood of the Lamb, not only sin but all its baggage will be absent.

Moreover, we will be his people and he will be our God. Heaven's photo, if one were taken, would show us standing right next to God. He would be looking down at us with a smile, and we would be beaming up at him with the unmistakable look of love. Heaven will be a step-by-step walk with God, in contrast to the straying course we often take here on earth. In heaven we will see his loving face, in contrast to the weak images we now hold in our imaginations. Just think, we will never be separated from him again. Imagine what it will be like to see, with both body and soul, the one who is loveliest to our eyes, dearest to our hearts, and most precious to our souls. Imagine what it will be like never again to have that glorious sight blurred by sin

Yes, tell me what it's like on the other side. More important, keep telling me about Jesus, the only way there.

Prayer

Thank you, dear Savior, for dressing me for heaven with your righteousness. Comfort me and cheer me with the joyous sight that waits for me there. Cradle me in your arms, and carry me safely to that place in glory. I ask this for the sake of your mercy and love. Amen.

22

LORD, WHY DON'T YOU TAKE ME?

I desire to depart and be with Christ, which is better
by far.

Philippians 1:23 (NIV)

"Please, pray that the Lord take me," Emma pleaded. For
her, the joys of life were long past. The days of bearing the
cross of her incurable disease had been numerous and
painful. "I won't do that," answered her pastor, "if you're
complaining about what God is sending and only impa-
tiently wanting to get out from under it. But if you want the
Lord to take you to heaven because you're eager to taste the
joys you'll find there, we can pray that way." So they prayed
that way, and ended their prayer with the words "Not my
will but yours be done."

The apostle Paul penned a similar prayer for our use. His
feet were still on this earth as he bore his heavy crosses. But
his eyes were on heaven. Because he knew what was waiting for him in heaven, he could hardly wait to get there. His
heart yearned to depart and enter the better life.

Notice how Paul talked about death. He didn't call it
the Grim Reaper, whose relentless scythe cuts us down. He
didn't label it the "king of terrors," whose icy grip sends
shivers down our spines. For him death meant to depart
and be with Christ. It meant leaving the things that are

temporary and torn by trouble to enjoy the treasures that are permanent and that come with peace. As a result, he viewed death as triumph rather than tragedy, as the beginning rather than the end. "Better by far" is the way he described that heavenly existence. "I desire to depart" is the way he expressed his yearning.

Christians yearn for heaven as little children yearn for Christmas. They know what is waiting for them at Jesus' side. And they can hardly wait to experience those joys in full. On some days during our walk through life, that yearning is stronger than on others. As death approaches, the intensity of the yearning heats up. A prayer for God to take us to heaven is not wrong. What could be wrong with the desire to depart and be with Christ? What could be wrong with the desire to see the Savior's face and to share his glory? What could be wrong with the desire to leave behind all the debris of this life and to live the sin-free, pain-free, death-free life with the Prince of life in heaven?

Please take me home, Lord. Nevertheless, not my will but yours be done.

Prayer

Lord, you know the pains of my life and the anguish of my soul. You also know how eager I am to leave this world of tears and to come home to you in heaven. So please understand my prayer. Help me bear my cross and bow to your will—and to be ready to depart when you call. Amen.

23

LORD, WALK WITH ME

Even though I walk through the valley of the shadow
of death, I will fear no evil, for you are with me; your
rod and your staff, they comfort me.

Psalm 23:4 (NIV)

Whether it's been sneaking up on me for days or has
suddenly just appeared before me, death is at the door. The
green pastures have turned into parched desert; the still
waters into raging waves. In death, as never before, I need
the assurance David offers so beautifully in his psalm. I
need to know that the Shepherd walks with me.

Please, Lord, remind me that the valley lying before me
is no longer filled with death—just its shadow. And like a
shadow, death can only scare me, not scar me. My Shepherd
protects me. On Calvary he walked through the actual valley of death. He took all the pains that sin had attached to
death and abolished them forever. Because he paid for my
sins, I don't have to stay in the valley. I can walk right
through it. The shadows may be frightening, the fog dense,
but behind the shadow there is always light. At the end of
the valley, heaven's eternal light shines, waiting for me.

Please, Lord, remind me also that you didn't say, "Go
ahead, start the journey. I'll be waiting for you at the other
end of the valley." Instead, you promised, "I'll be with you.

You won't be walking alone." Help me see that you are walking, not behind me, not even beside me, but ahead of me. You lead because you know the way. You've walked through this valley before. The wounds that I see as you hold my hand assure me that your way is true. As you guide my steps over this somber path, your rod and staff give me comfort. What enemy can stand up against your power? Like the shepherd's rod that chases the wolves away, your power will keep the devil at bay. Like the shepherd's staff that pulls the sheep closer, your love will not let me stray. My journey through the dark valley will be safe. "You are with me."

When David spoke of the comfort he received from your rod and staff, he used a word that means to "breathe easily." When I see you leading me through the valley of the shadow of death, I can breathe easily because you are with me.

Prayer

Lord, hear my prayer and walk with me. Amen.

24

Lord, Give Me Safe Sleep

I will lie down and sleep in peace, for you alone, O Lord, make me dwell in safety.

Psalm 4:8 (NIV)

The psalmist David was writing at the end of another hard day of life. What he had to say about lying down in safety and sleeping in peace fits well also for the hardest day of life, that final day we know as death. The Scriptures use the term *sleep* 14 times to describe the death of a believer. Speaking of Jairus' daughter, Jesus said, "The child is not dead but asleep" (Mark 5:39). When Lazarus died, Jesus told his disciples, "Lazarus has fallen asleep" (John 11:11). In Acts chapter 7, we read that Stephen fell asleep. And Paul wrote to the Thessalonians about those who fall asleep.

For a believer, death is like a rest-bringing sleep. Perhaps that picture brings to mind our younger days. Mother would tuck us into our beds at night and kiss away the cares of the day. That picture also reminds us of nights when we crawled into our beds seeking a brief respite from the rigors of the day. Sleep is a good description of death. A believer's death offers rest. Rest from all the cares brought into the world by sin. Rest from the sorrows and sufferings, the pains and problems, and the toils and troubles that only get heavier as the years increase. For a believer, death offers an even greater rest. It offers rest from the spiritual warfare that soldiers of the cross face. Every single day the commander of hell and his legions march out against us. Only in death is the battle over and the victory won.

For a believer, death is like sleep in another way. When we fall asleep on our pillows at night, we do not cease to exist. When we die, we don't cease to exist either. At the time of death, a believer's body no longer houses the soul, but the soul is carried to heaven to be forever with the Lord. So Jesus could promise the dying thief, "Today you will be with me in paradise" (Luke 23:43). That promise was behind Paul's desire to be "away from the body and at home with the Lord" (2 Corinthians 5:8). Death brings the best rest of all—sweet rest with the Savior in heaven. There we will see him face-to-face. We will carry the victor's palm. We will wear the garments washed in his blood. And we will join with all the saints and angels to sing his praises.

But death brings rest only for believers. Only those who know and trust God's great love for them in Jesus the Savior can look forward to such rest. Only they can lie down in peace and sleep in safety on death's bed. And believers know that only our gracious Lord can create such trust in the human heart. So, in the hour of death, we pray, "Lord, give me such safe sleep."

Prayer

Ah, Lord, you know how much I want that rest. How ready I am to leave the sins and sorrows of this life behind. Hold me close with the promises of your Word. Let me feel the Savior's arms around me so that, as his child, I may close my eyes in peace and safety. Amen.

25

LORD, TAKE ME HOME

"In my Father's house are many rooms; if it were not so, I would have told you. I am going there to prepare a place for you. And if I go and prepare a place for you, I will come back and take you to be with me that you also may be where I am."

John 14:2,3 (NIV)

"My Father's house," Jesus calls heaven. Can there be a more comforting picture than this? It reminds me how, as a child, I found warmth and security in my parents' home. When I was sick, there was no better place to be than in my own bed. The highlight of my school day was coming back home. And though my own children have now reached middle age, they still enjoy sitting around the dinner table in our home. Such a homecoming is waiting for me in my Father's house. Death is taking me home.

In that home are many rooms. As I listen closely, I realize that Jesus means this to be my permanent dwelling place. How different from the temporary motel this earth is. Life here on earth is really just a brief journey to heaven: heaven will be my permanent home. Jesus said that his Father's house has many rooms and that he was going to prepare one for me. He, whose love singled me out as an object of his eternal grace, has a room waiting for me in the Father's house. He has stenciled my name on the door, decorated the walls with the dazzling paint of his holiness, and signed a permanent lease with his own blood. He is now holding a room in my name.

And he has promised, "I will come back and take you to be with me." Sometimes when a mother leaves her child at a baby-sitter's house, she has to quiet the child's anxiety. "Don't cry. I'll be back soon." In the same way, the Savior promises, "I will come back." He promises even more, "I will take you to be with me that you also may be where I am." What comfort for my tears! What an answer for my fears! I have his promise that he will take me to live with him in my Father's house above. With his risen, living, nail-pierced hands, Jesus holds open the doors to the Father's house above. He holds them open for me.

Lord Jesus, take me home. Let me stay for eternity.

Prayer

Lord, I don't know how much time I have left or how many more breaths I will take in this passing world. Show me the Father's house above and the room you have prepared for me. In my last moment, hold me by the hand and lead me so that I reach home safely. For the sake of your love, I ask this. Amen.